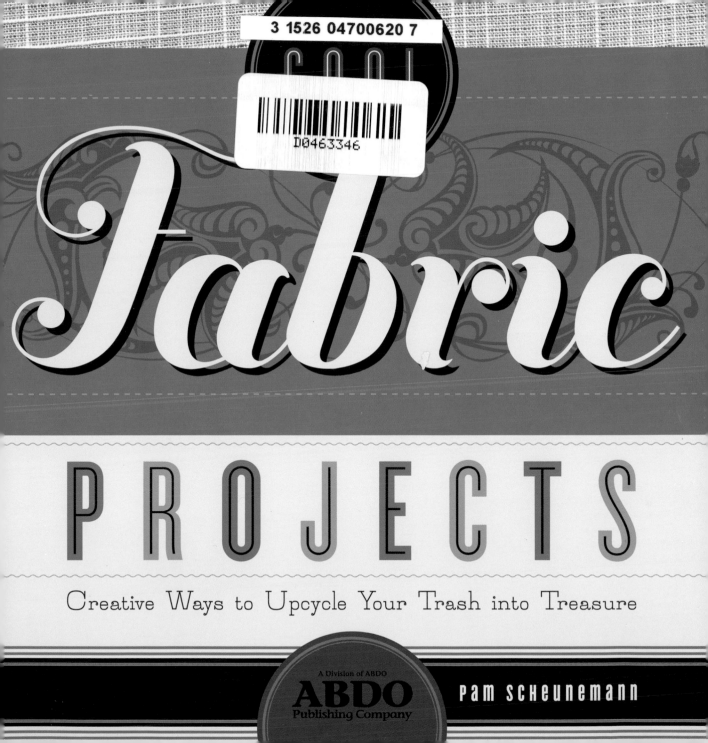

Cool Fabric PROJECTS

Creative Ways to Upcycle Your Trash into Treasure

A Division of ABDO
ABDO Publishing Company

PAM SCHEUNEMANN

visit us at www.abdopublishing.com

Published by ABDO Publishing Company, a division of ABDO, P.O. Box 398166, Minneapolis, Minnesota 55439. Copyright © 2013 by Abdo Consulting Group, Inc. International copyrights reserved in all countries. No part of this book may be reproduced in any form without written permission from the publisher. Checkerboard Library™ is a trademark and logo of ABDO Publishing Company.

Printed in the United States of America, North Mankato, Minnesota
062012
092012

♻ PRINTED ON RECYCLED PAPER

DESIGN AND PRODUCTION: ANDERS HANSON, MIGHTY MEDIA, INC.
SERIES EDITOR: LIZ SALZMANN
PHOTO CREDITS: SHUTTERSTOCK

The following manufacturers/names appearing in this book are trademarks: Aleene's® Tacky Glue®, Elmer's®, Fiskars®, Rapala®, Reynolds®, Sharpie®, Singer®, Sunbeam®, Tulip® Soft Fabric Paint™

LIBRARY OF CONGRESS CATALOGING-IN-PUBLICATION DATA

Scheunemann, Pam, 1955-
  Cool fabric projects : creative ways to upcycle your trash into treasure / Pam Scheunemann.
      p. cm. -- (Cool trash to treasure)
  Includes index.
  ISBN 978-1-61783-432-5
  1. Textile crafts--Juvenile literature. I. Title.
TT712.S378 2013
746--dc23
                           2011052198

TABLE of CONTENTS

Trash to Treasure	4
A Fresh Look at Fabric	6
Tools & Materials	8
Earbud Wire Covers	10
Funky Yarn Scarf	12
Fabric Scrap Cards	14
Cool Coiled Baskets	16
Paint Splatter T-Shirt	20
Tie It, You'll Like It!	22
Felted Wool Headband	24
Conclusion	30
Glossary	31
Web Sites	31
Index	32

TRASH TO Treasure

THE SKY'S THE LIMIT

The days of throwing everything in the trash are long over. Recycling has become a part of everyday life. To recycle means to use something again or to find a new use for it. By creating treasures out of trash, we are also *upcycling*. This is a term used to **describe** making useful items out of things that may have been thrown away.

Do you have a stained T-shirt? What about those pants you've outgrown? Do you have a favorite blouse that's seen better days? Did your wool sweater shrink in the wash? Don't toss them, upcycle them! There are many things you can do with old clothes, scraps of yarn, and **fabric**. See what you can come up with. The sky's the limit!

Permission and Safety

- Always get **permission** before making any type of craft at home.

- Ask if you can use the tools and materials needed.

- Ask for help when you need it.

- Be careful when using knives, scissors, or other sharp objects.

Be Prepared

- Read the entire activity before you begin.

- Make sure you have everything you need to do the project.

- Keep your work area neat and organized.

- Follow the directions carefully.

- Clean up after you are finished for the day.

In this book you'll find great ideas to upcycle different kinds of **fabric** and yarn. Make them just like they appear here or use your own ideas. You can make them for yourself or as gifts for others. These projects use easy-to-find tools and materials.

FABRIC

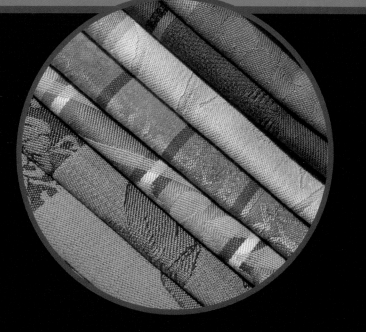

There are many sources for **fabric** and yarn. Maybe you like to knit, **crochet**, **quilt**, or sew. Or maybe someone you know does. If so, you can use the leftover yarn and fabric scraps. And don't forget about your old clothes. If they can't be **donated**, reuse the material! These things can be upcycled.

If you can sew, there are many things you can make. The projects in this book require very little sewing.

Yarn scraps can be used in many ways. Old wool sweaters can be made into felt. Crafting with felt is fun and easy too!

Fabric

- PURSES
- BASKETS
- BOOK COVERS
- TOTE BAGS
- GREETING CARDS
- DECORATED SWEATSHIRTS

Yarn

- SCARVES
- HATS
- EARBUD COVERS
- BRACELETS
- CANDLE MATS

WORKING WITH FABRIC

- Wash old clothes before you use them in a craft project.
- If possible, get some **fabric** scissors. They are made for cutting fabric. They work much better than general-purpose scissors. Don't use them on anything but fabric or they will get dull quickly.

TOOLS & MATERIALS

BEADS

BROWN PAPER BAG

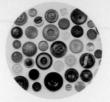

BUTTONS

CARD STOCK

CLEAR FISHING LINE

COTTON CLOTHESLINE

CRAFT FELT

DECORATIVE PAPER PUNCH

EARBUDS

EMBROIDERY FLOSS

EMBROIDERY NEEDLE

ENVELOPES

FABRIC PAINT

FABRIC SCISSORS

FABRIC SCRAPS

FREEZER PAPER

If you don't know what something is, turn back to these pages!

GLUE STICK

IRON

MASKING TAPE

MEASURING TAPE

NEWSPAPER

OLD 100% WOOL SWEATER

OLD TIES

PAINTBRUSH

RULER

SELF-ADHESIVE HOOK AND LOOP DOTS

STAINED T-SHIRT

STRAIGHT PINS

TACKY GLUE

WAX PAPER

WIDE-EYE PLASTIC NEEDLE

YARN SCRAPS

- EARBUDS
- MASKING TAPE
- YARN SCRAPS
- SCISSORS
- TACKY GLUE

EARBUD WIRE COVERS

Jazz up your earbud wires!

1   Tape the end of the earbud wire to a flat surface. Tie a piece of yarn around the wire near the tape. Tie it with the knot in the middle of the yarn so the ends are even.

2   Bring the left end over the wire. Wrap the right end over the left end and under the wire. Then bring it up between the wire and the left end of the yarn. Pull the knot tight.

3   Now do the opposite. Bring the right end of the yarn over the wire. Wrap the left end over the right end and under the wire. Then bring it up between the wire and the right end of the yarn. Pull the knot tight.

4   Keep repeating steps 2 and 3 until the wire is covered. Add more yarn if necessary. Just tie the new yarn to the ends of the old yarn. Use double knots and cut off the ends close to the knots.

5   When the wire is covered, tie the yarn in a double knot around the wire. Trim the ends. Put a dab of glue on the knot so it won't come undone.

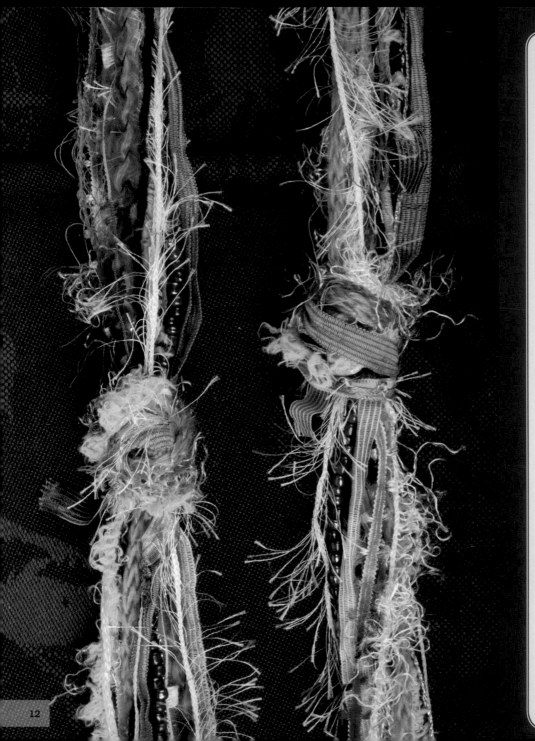

- **YARN SCRAPS (ABOUT 70 INCHES (127–178 CM) LONG)**

- **REGULAR SCISSORS**

- **BEADS (OPTIONAL)**

- **CLEAR FISHING LINE (OPTIONAL)**

FUNKY Yarn Scarf

Yarn leftovers made lovely!

1. Decide how long you want the **scarf** to be. Then add 15 inches (38 cm). Cut all of the pieces of yarn to the total length. If you aren't sure how long to make it, start a little longer. You can cut it shorter later if necessary.

2. If you want to add a strand of beads, string the beads on the fishing line. Make it the same length as the yarn. Tie a knot in each end of the fishing line so the beads won't fall off.

3. Gather the yarn scraps and the string of beads together. Gently twist them to make a thick rope. Tie it into a knot in the middle.

4. Tie knots about halfway between the center and each end. Then tie knots about 6 inches (15 cm) from each end.

5. Trim the ends to make them even. Enjoy wearing your new scarf!

STUFF YOU'LL NEED

- **BLANK CARD STOCK**

- **FABRIC SCRAPS**

- **FABRIC SCISSORS**

- **REGULAR SCISSORS**

- **DECORATIVE PUNCHES**

- **TACKY GLUE**

- **PAINTBRUSH**

- **ENVELOPES**

- **RIBBON**

- **STACK OF BOOKS**

FABRIC SCRAP CARDS

Give a stack of these as a gift!

1   Measure the envelope. Fold a piece of card stock in half. Cut it so the card is a little smaller than the envelope. Put the card in the envelope to make sure it fits. Take it back out.

2   Select a decorative punch. Punch holes in the front of the card.

3   Hold the card over different fabric scraps. Find a pattern that looks good through the holes in the card. Cut a piece of fabric that covers the holes. But make sure it doesn't stick out past the edges of the card.

4   Open the card. Put small dots of glue around the holes. Do not use too much glue. Press the fabric over the glue. Cut another piece of card stock to cover the back of the fabric. Glue it over the fabric. Add ribbon or other decorations.

5   Put the card under a **stack** of books until the glue dries. This keeps the card from warping.

STUFF YOU'LL NEED

- **COTTON CLOTHESLINE**

- **TAPE**

- **REGULAR SCISSORS**

- **FABRIC SCRAPS**

- **FABRIC SCISSORS**

- **RULER**

- **WIDE-EYE PLASTIC NEEDLE**

- **GLUE STICK**

- **TACKY GLUE**

COOL COILED BASKETS

These baskets hold it all!

1. Wrap tape around the end of the clothesline. Cut the cord right at the end of the tape. This keeps the end from **fraying**.

2. Use fabric scissors to cut strips of fabric. They should be ½ inch (1 cm) wide. Make the strips as long as possible.

3. Put a strip of fabric through the eye of the needle. Pull it through about 2 inches (3 cm).

Continued on the next page

alternate colors

4 Use the glue stick to put glue on the back of the long end of the strip. Cover about 1 inch (3 cm) of the strip. Wrap the glued end around the end of the clothesline.

5 Wrap the fabric tightly around the clothesline at an angle. **Overlap** the edges slightly with each wrap. Cover about 2 inches (5 cm) of the clothesline.

6 Make a tight coil with the wrapped end of the clothesline. Hold it together and put the needle through the center of the coil. Pull the strip all the way through. Pull the fabric tight.

7 Hold the coil tightly. Keep wrapping the fabric around the clothesline. Every inch (3 cm) or so, add more of the clothesline to the coil. Attach it by pushing the needle through a gap in the coil. Pull the strip all the way through.

8   When you get to the end of a fabric strip, glue the end around the clothesline. Put another strip on the needle. Glue the end around the clothesline where the previous strip ended.

9   Keep wrapping and coiling. Stop when the coil is as large as you want the bottom of the basket to be.

10 Start creating the sides of the basket. Guide the wrapped clothesline on top of the outer coil instead of next to it. Attach the clothesline like in step 7. Widen the basket by moving each new coil out slightly as you attach it to the previous coil. This takes a bit of practice.

11 To make a handle. pull the wrapped clothesline away from the top coil. Keep it pulled away while attaching the clothesline to the top coil.

12 When the basket is the size you want it, cut the clothesline. Wrap a piece of tape around the end. Use the glue stick to put glue on the end of the fabric strip. Completely cover the end of the clothesline with fabric. Cut off any extra fabric. Glue the end of the clothesline to the basket with Tacky Glue.

STUFF YOU'LL NEED

- NEWSPAPER
- BROWN PAPER BAG
- REGULAR SCISSORS
- MARKER
- DOUBLE-SIDED TAPE
- STAINED T-SHIRT
- FABRIC PAINT
- SMALL BOWL
- WATER
- PAINTBRUSH

PAINT SPLATTER T-SHIRT

Upcycle a stained T-shirt!

1   Spread newspaper over your work area. If possible, do this activity outside. There will be a lot of **splatter**!

2   Cut open a brown paper bag. Draw a design to cover the stain on the T-shirt. Poke the scissors through the bag inside the design. Cut from there to the edge of the design. Then cut out the design.

3   Flip the bag over. Put double-sided tape around the edges of the cutout area. Spread the T-shirt out on the newspaper. Turn the bag back over. Place it on the shirt so the stain shows inside the cutout area. Press around the edges of the design. Use more newspaper to cover any part of the shirt that sticks out past the sides of the bag.

4   Put some fabric paint in a bowl. Add a little water to thin the paint. Dip the paintbrush in the paint. Flick the brush toward the cutout area of the bag. Repeat until the shirt showing through the design is covered with paint. Try using more than one color. Let the paint dry completely before removing the paper bag.

STUFF YOU'LL NEED

- OLD TIE
- RULER
- FABRIC SCISSORS
- WAX PAPER
- TACKY GLUE
- STRAIGHT PINS
- MASKING TAPE
- SELF-ADHESIVE HOOK AND LOOP DOTS
- BUTTON, NEEDLE, AND THREAD (OPTIONAL)

TIE IT, YOU'LL LIKE IT!

Make a pouch for a phone or glasses

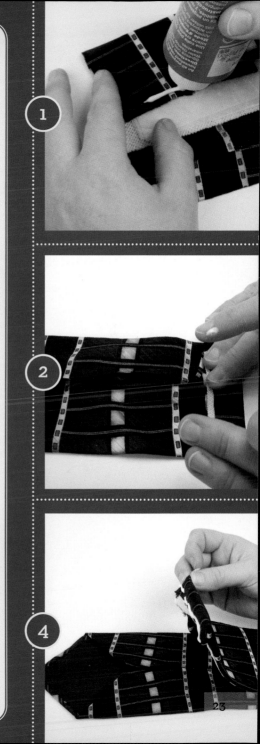

1. Lay the tie out flat. Cut the tie 16 inches (41 cm) from the larger point. Cut off the label. Open the tie by cutting any threads in the center. Cut a piece of wax paper to fit inside the tie. Glue the tie closed with the wax paper inside.

2. Put glue along the cut end of the tie. Fold it over about 1 inch (3 cm). Pin the fold in place until the glue dries. Then remove the pins and wax paper.

3. Fold the glued end up to where the center seam starts. Put a small piece of masking tape on the table to mark the fold line.

4. Unfold the tie. Make sure not to move it! Put glue along each side from the glued end to the tape mark. Put glue on the glued end too. Fold the tie again and press the edges firmly. Let the glue dry.

5. Put a hook and loop dot together. Take the backing off one side. Put the dot near the point of the tie. Remove the backing from the other side. Fold the point to make a flap. Press the dot on top of the end you folded up in step 4. If you want, sew a decorative button on the outside of the flap.

- OLD 100% WOOL SWEATER

- WASHING MACHINE

- CLOTHES DRYER

- MEASURING TAPE

- FREEZER PAPER

- MARKER

- RULER

- REGULAR SCISSORS

- IRON

- FABRIC SCISSORS

- SELF-ADHESIVE HOOK AND LOOP DOTS

- CRAFT FELT (OPTIONAL)

- EMBROIDERY NEEDLE

- EMBROIDERY FLOSS

- BUTTON

- NEEDLE AND THREAD (OPTIONAL)

FELTED WOOL HEADBAND

Give new life to an old sweater!

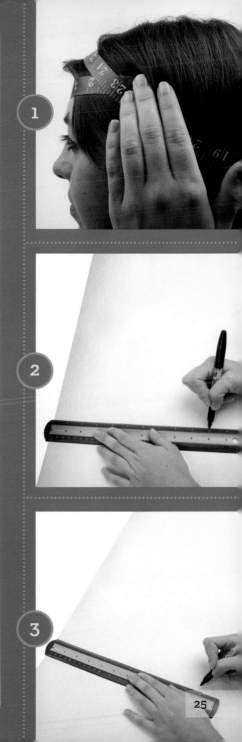

MAKING FELTED WOOL

Wash the wool sweater in the washing machine using hot water. Then dry it in the dryer using the hottest setting. Check to see if it feels like felt. If it still seems more like woven yarn than felt, wash and dry it again. Repeat until the sweater feels like felt.

1. Wrap the measuring tape around your head as if you were wearing a headband. Add 1 inch (3 cm) to the measurement. That's the total measurement. Write it down.

2. Tear off a piece of freezer paper. It should be a little longer than the total measurement. Fold it in half crosswise. Draw a straight line from the middle of the fold to the opposite edge.

3. Divide the total measurement in half. Measure that far along the line starting at the fold. Make a mark.

Continued on the next page

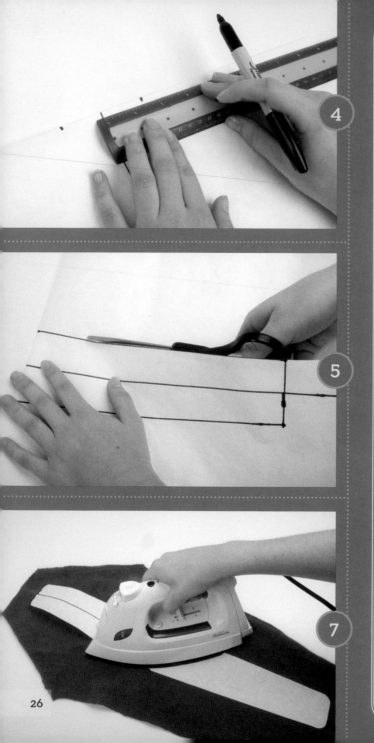

4 Make marks on the fold 1¹/2 inches (4 cm) on each side of the line. Make marks 1 inch (3 cm) on each side of the mark you made in step 3.

5 Use a ruler to draw a straight line between the two marks on the right side of the line. Do the same on the left side. Draw a line between the marks that are not on the fold. Cut along the outer lines. Make sure you cut through both layers. Round off the corners on the end away from the fold. Unfold the paper. This is the headband pattern.

6 Wrap the pattern around your head to see if it fits. The ends should **overlap** about 1 inch (3 cm). It's okay if it's a little bigger. But if it's too small, make a new pattern using a larger measurement.

7 Place the pattern on the wool felt. Lay it waxy side down. Iron it so it sticks to the felt.

8 Use fabric scissors to cut the felt around the pattern. Remove the pattern. Wrap the felt around your head. Does it fit? Do the ends **overlap** about 1 inch (3 cm)? Is it wider than you want it to be? You can make it smaller by trimming the edges.

9 Put a hook and loop dot together. Take the backing off one side. Put it about 1/2 inch (1 cm) from one of the ends. Remove the backing from the other side. Wrap the headband around your head. Press the end with the hook and loop dot firmly against the other end.

10 Cut a flower and some leaves out of felt. If you need more colors than you have sweaters, use scraps of craft felt.

11 Use the blanket **stitch** to sew on the flower. This stitch is **described** on the next page. You could also stitch around the edges of the headband. If you want, sew a decorative button over the hook and loop dot.

27

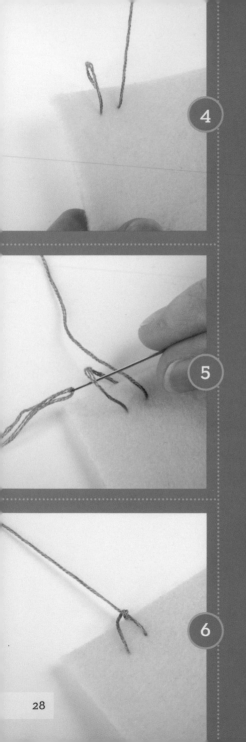

How to do the blanket stitch

The blanket **stitch** is an embroidery stitch that looks nice on both sides. It is often used around the edges of a project, such as a blanket! You can use floss the same color as the felt. Or choose a different color that will show against the felt.

1   Cut a piece of embroidery floss about 2 feet (61 cm) long. Separate out three strands of the floss. (See opposite page.)

2   Put the ends of the strands together and thread them through the needle. Pull them about one-quarter of the way through the needle. Tie a knot at the end of the longer side.

3   Position the needle behind the felt about 1/4 inch (.6 cm) from the edge. Push the needle up through the felt. Pull it until the knot hits the back of the felt.

4   Move the needle about 1/4 inch (.6 cm) to the right of where the thread came up. Push the needle up through the felt again. Pull the floss through most of the way. Leave a little loop.

5   Put the needle through the loop from left to right.

6   Pull it snug.

7   Repeat steps 4 through 6.

8   When you reach the end of the thread or the
    end of the felt, you'll need to make a knot.
    Push the needle through the top of the last
    stitch. Before pulling it all the way, put it
    through the loop you just made. Pull tight to
    make a knot.

9   To hide the end, run the needle from the top
    edge of the felt in about ¼ inch (.6 cm).
    Pull it through. Cut the thread off right next
    to the felt.

Separating embroidery floss

There are six strands of thread in embroidery floss.
The strands must be separated before use.

1   Roll the end of the floss between your finger
    and thumb.

2   Separate the ends of the strands.

3   Grasp one strand and gently pull it away
    from the others. Repeat until you have three
    strands.

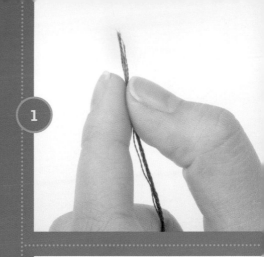

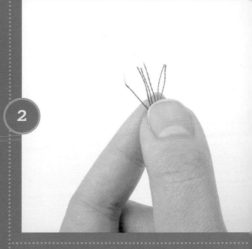

29

CONCLUSION

Now you know what upcycling is all about. What hidden gems do you have around your house? Do you have relatives who need their **attic** cleaned? What about **garage** and yard sales? Are there **thrift stores** and reuse centers near you? These are all great sources for materials that you can upcycle!

There are many benefits to upcycling. You can make some really great stuff for yourself or gifts for your family and friends. You can save useful things from going into the trash. And the best part is, you don't have to spend a lot of money doing it!

So keep your eyes and ears open for new ideas. There are many Web sites that are all about recycling and upcycling. You might find ideas on TV or in magazines. There are endless ways that you can make something beautiful and useful from **discarded** materials. Remember, the sky is the limit!

GLOSSARY

ATTIC – a room right under the roof of a building.

CROCHET – to use a special needle with a hook to weave things out of yarn or thread.

DESCRIBE – to tell about something with words or pictures.

DISCARD – to throw away.

DONATE – to give a gift in order to help others.

FRAY – to unravel or become worn at the edge.

GARAGE – a room or building that cars are kept in. A *garage sale* is a sale that takes place in a garage.

OVERLAP – to lie partly on top of something.

PERMISSION – when a person in charge says it's okay to do something.

QUILT – to sew a blanket that has two layers of cloth with a warm filling such as wool or cotton in the middle.

SCARF – a long piece of cloth worn around the neck for decoration or to keep warm.

SPLATTER – drops of liquid that have been thrown or scattered around.

STACK – 1. a pile of things placed one on top of the other. 2. to put things in a pile.

STITCH – a small length of thread left in fabric by moving the needle in and out one time.

THRIFT STORE – a store that sells used items, especially one that is run by a charity.

Web sites

To learn more about cool craft projects, visit ABDO Publishing Company on the World Wide Web at www.abdopublishing.com. Web sites about creative ways for upcycling trash are featured on our Book Links page. These links are routinely monitored and updated to provide the most current information available.

INDEX

B

Baskets, project for, 16–19

Blanket stitch, 27, 28–29

C

Cards, project for, 14–15

D

Directions, reading and following, 5

E

Earbud wires, project for, 10–11

Embroidery, 28–29

Embroidery floss, separating, 29

F

Fabric

projects using, 4, 6, 7, 14–15, 16–19, 20–21, 22–23, 24–27

scissors for, 7

sources of, 4, 5, 6, 7

Felted wool, 24

G

Gifts, making, 5, 30

H

Headband, project for, 24–27

P

Permission, to do projects, 5

Pouch, project for, 22–23

Preparing, to do projects, 5

R

Recycling, 4

S

Safety guidelines, for projects, 5

Scarf, project for, 12–13

Scissors

for fabric, 7

safe use of, 5

Sewing, 7

Sharp objects, safe use of, 5

T

T-shirt, project for, 20–21

Tools and materials

list of, 8–9

organizing, 5

permission to use, 5

sources of, 4, 5, 6, 7, 30

U

Upcycling, 4–5

benefits of, 30

definition of, 4

projects for, 4–5, 7, 30, 31

W

Web sites, about projects, 30, 31

Work area, organizing and cleaning, 5

Y

Yarn

projects using, 4, 6, 7, 10–11, 12–13

sources of, 4, 5, 6, 7